Samuel French Acting Edition

The Apollo of Bellac

by Maurice Valency

SAMUELFRENCH.COM   SAMUELFRENCH.CO.UK

Copyright © 1954, 1982 by Maurice Valency
All Rights Reserved

THE APOLLO OF BELLAC is fully protected under the copyright laws of the United States of America, the British Commonwealth, including Canada, and all other countries of the Copyright Union. All rights, including professional and amateur stage productions, recitation, lecturing, public reading, motion picture, radio broadcasting, television and the rights of translation into foreign languages are strictly reserved.

ISBN 978-0-573-62017-1

www.SamuelFrench.com
www.SamuelFrench.co.uk

FOR PRODUCTION ENQUIRIES

UNITED STATES AND CANADA
Info@SamuelFrench.com
1-866-598-8449

UNITED KINGDOM AND EUROPE
Plays@SamuelFrench.co.uk
020-7255-4302

Each title is subject to availability from Samuel French, depending upon country of performance. Please be aware that *THE APOLLO OF BELLAC* may not be licensed by Samuel French in your territory. Professional and amateur producers should contact the nearest Samuel French office or licensing partner to verify availability.

CAUTION: Professional and amateur producers are hereby warned that *THE APOLLO OF BELLAC* is subject to a licensing fee. Publication of this play(s) does not imply availability for performance. Both amateurs and professionals considering a production are strongly advised to apply to Samuel French before starting rehearsals, advertising, or booking a theatre. A licensing fee must be paid whether the title(s) is presented for charity or gain and whether or not admission is charged. Professional/Stock licensing fees are quoted upon application to Samuel French.

No one shall make any changes in this title(s) for the purpose of production. No part of this book may be reproduced, stored in a retrieval system, or transmitted in any form, by any means, now known or yet to be invented, including mechanical, electronic, photocopying, recording, videotaping, or otherwise, without the prior written permission of the publisher. No one shall upload this title(s), or part of this title(s), to any social media websites.

For all enquiries regarding motion picture, television, and other media rights, please contact Samuel French.

Please refer to page 39 for further copyright information.

The Man from Bellac is not Apollo. The Man from Bellac is a little shabby fellow who doesn't know where his next meal is coming from. He is a vagabond and a poet, therefore an inventor. He dreams things up, but he does nothing and he has nothing. He was cast very sensibly on the Ford Omnibus television program, when Claude Dauphin played the role—a fine character-actor, not a matinee idol. The Man from Bellac must evoke Apollo, but visually he must remain the shabby little figure throughout the play. The moment he is cast as a big beautiful man with curly ringlets, the play is spoiled.

MAURICE VALENCY

THE APOLLO OF BELLAC
STORY OF THE PLAY

Here, in long one-act form, is the quintessence of Giraudoux' extraordinary imagination and style. The scene is set in an Office of Inventions (Typical invention: a book that reads itself). A shy girl comes for a job. She is ignored, until a nondescript little man from the town of Bellac comes to her aid. He demonstrates that she can have her way with any man if she will, upon meeting him, declare that he is handsome and compare him to the statue of the Apollo of Bellac (nonexistent). This she does, beginning hesitantly with the clerk and working up most successfully to the Chairman of the Board. The play is alive with wry and trenchant observations. Moral: "The best career for a female is to be a woman."

THE APOLLO OF BELLAC

CAST

(9 males; 3 females)

AGNES
THERESE
THE CLERK
THE MAN
THE VICE-PRESIDENT
MR. CRACHETON
MR. LEPEDURA
MR. RASEMUTTE
MR. SCHULTZ
THE PRESIDENT
CHEVREDENT
THE CHAIRMAN OF THE BOARD

The Apollo of Bellac

SCENE: *The reception room of The International Bureau of Inventions, S.A.*

This is a large, well-appointed room on the second floor of a magnificent office building in Paris. The French windows are open and afford us a view of tree-tops. There is an elaborate crystal chandelier hanging from the ceiling. The morning sun plays upon it. On a pedestal large enough to conceal a man a bust of Archimedes is set. Four doors open off the room. Three of them are marked Private. These lead into the office of the President, Right, and the First Vice-President rear Right, and the Directors' Conference Room rear Left. The effect is French and very elegant, perhaps a trifle oppressive in its opulence. (See ground plan back of book.)

Behind a period desk sits the RECEPTION CLERK. *The desk has an ivory telephone and a row of signal lights. It has also a period blotter on which the clerk is writing something in an appointment book. The Clerk is well on in years and his face makes one think of a caricature by Daumier.*

TIME: *Autumn in Paris. The present or shortly before.*

AT RISE: THE CLERK *is writing with a meticulous air. The outer door opens.* AGNES *comes in timidly from outer door, and stands in front of the desk.* THE CLERK *does not look up.*

AGNES. Er—

THE APOLLO OF BELLAC

CLERK. Yes?

AGNES. Is this the International Bureau of Inventions, Incorporated?

CLERK. Yes.

AGNES. Could I please see the Chairman of the Board?

CLERK. *(Looks up)* The Chairman of the Board? No one sees the Chairman of the Board.

AGNES. Oh.

(The outer door opens again. THERESE *sweeps into the room. She is blonde, shapely, thirty-five, dressed in expensive mink.* CLERK *rises respectfully.)*

CLERK. Good morning, Madame.
THERESE. Is the President in?
CLERK. Yes, Madame. Of course.

*(*THERESE *walks haughtily to President's door.* CLERK *opens it for her and closes it behind her. He goes back to his desk where* AGNES *is waiting.)*

AGNES. Could I see the President?
CLERK. No one sees the President.
AGNES. But I have—
CLERK. What type of invention? Major? Intermediate? Minor?
AGNES. I beg pardon?
CLERK. Assistant Secretary to the Third Vice-President. Come back Tuesday. Name?
AGNES. My name?
CLERK. You have a name, I presume?

*(*THE MAN FROM BELLAC *appears suddenly from outer door. He is nondescript, mercurial, shabby.)*

MAN. Yes. The young lady has a name. But what permits you to conclude that the young lady's invention is as minor as all that?

CLERK. Who are you?

MAN. What chiefly distinguishes the inventor is modesty. You should know that by now. Pride is the invention of non-inventors.

(A STREET SINGER, *accompanied by violin and accordian, begins "La Seine" outside the windows.* CLERK *crosses to close them.*)

AGNES. *(To the* MAN) Thanks very much, but—

MAN. To the characteristic modesty of the inventor, the young lady adds the charming modesty of her sex— *(He smiles at* AGNES) But—

(CLERK *closes one of the windows.*)

how can you be sure, you, that she has not brought us at last the invention which is destined to transform the modern world?

CLERK. *(Closes the other window)* For world-transformations it's the Second Vice President. Mondays ten to twelve.

MAN. Today is Tuesday.

CLERK. Now how can I help that?

MAN. So! While all humanity awaits with anguish the discovery which will at last utilize the moon's gravitation for the removal of corns, and when we have every reason to believe that in all likelihood Mademoiselle— Mademoiselle?

AGNES. Agnes.

MAN. Mademoiselle Agnes has this discovery in her handbag— You tell her to come back Monday.

CLERK. *(Nervously)* There is going to be a Directors' meeting in just a few minutes. The Chairman of the Board is coming. I must beg you to be quiet.

MAN. I will not be quiet. I am quiet Mondays.

CLERK. Now, please. I don't want·any trouble.

MAN. And the Universal Vegetable? Five continents are languishing in the hope of the Universal Vegetable which will once and for all put an end to the ridiculous specialization of the turnip, the leek and the string-

THE APOLLO OF BELLAC 9

bean, which will be at one and the same time bread, meat, wine and coffee, and yield with equal facility cotton, potassium, ivory and wool. The Universal Vegetable which Paracelsus could not, and Burbank dared not, imagine! Yes, my friend. And while in this handbag, which with understandable concern she clutches to her charming bosom, the seeds of the Universal Vegetable await only the signal of your President to burst upon an expectant world, you say—come back Monday.

AGNES. Really, sir—

CLERK. If you wish an appointment for Monday, Mademoiselle—

MAN. She does not wish an appointment for Monday.

CLERK. *(Shrugs)* Then she can go jump in the lake.

MAN. What did you say?

CLERK. I said: She can go jump in the lake. Is that clear?

MAN. That's clear. Perfectly clear. As clear as it was to Columbus when—

(The BUZZER sounds on the CLERK's desk. A LIGHT flashes on.)

CLERK. Excuse me. *(He crosses to the VICE PRESIDENT's door, knocks and enters.)*

(MAN *smiles.* AGNES *smiles back wanly.*)

AGNES. But I'm not the inventor of the Universal Vegetable.

MAN. I know. I am.

AGNES. I'm just looking for a job.

MAN. Typist?

AGNES. Not really.

MAN. Stenographer?

AGNES. Not at all.

MAN Copy-reader, translator, book-keeper, editor, file-clerk—stop me when I come to it.

AGNES. You could go on like that for years before I could stop you.

MAN. Well then—your specialty? Charm? Coquetry, devotion, seduction, flirtation, passion, romance?

AGNES. That's getting warmer.

MAN. Splendid. The best career for a female is to be a woman.

AGNES. Yes, but—men frighten me.

MAN. Men frighten you?

AGNES. They make me feel weak all over.

MAN. That clerk frightens you?

AGNES. Clerks, presidents, janitors, soldiers. All a man has to do is to look at me, and I feel like a shoplifter caught in the act.

MAN. Caught in what act?

AGNES. I don't know.

MAN. Perhaps it's their clothes that frighten you. Their vests? Their trousers?

AGNES. *(Shakes her head)* I feel the same panic on the beach when they don't wear their trousers.

MAN. Perhaps you don't like men.

AGNES. Oh, no, I like them. I like their dog-like eyes, their hairiness, their big feet. And they have special organs which inspire tenderness in a woman—. Their Adam's apple, for instance, when they eat dinner or make speeches. But the moment they speak to me, I begin to tremble—

MAN. *(He looks appraisingly at her a moment)* You would like to stop trembling?

AGNES. Oh yes. But— *(She shrugs hopelessly.)*

MAN. Would you like me to teach you the secret?

AGNES. Secret?

MAN. Of not trembling before men. Of getting whatever you want out of them. Of making the directors jump, the presidents kneel and offer you diamonds?

AGNES. Are there such secrets?

MAN. One only. It is infallible.

AGNES. Will you really tell it to me?

MAN. Without this secret a girl has a bad time of it

THE APOLLO OF BELLAC

on this earth. With it, she becomes Empress of the World.

AGNES. Oh tell it to me quickly.

MAN. *(Peering about the room)* No one is listening?

AGNES. *(Whispers)* No one.

MAN. Tell them they're handsome.

AGNES. You mean, flatter them? Tell them they're handsome, intelligent, kind?

MAN. No. As for the intelligence and the kindness, they can shift for themselves. Tell them they're handsome.

AGNES. All?

MAN. All. The foolish, the wise, the modest, the vain, the young, the old. Say it to the professor of philosophy and he will give you a diploma. Say it to the butcher and he will give you a steak. Say it to the president here, and he will give you a job.

AGNES. But to say a thing like that, one has to know a person well—

MAN. Not at all. Say it right off. Say it before he has a chance even to open his mouth.

AGNES. But one doesn't say a thing like that before people.

MAN. Before people. Before all the world. The more witnesses, the better.

AGNES. But if they're not handsome—and for the most part they're not, you know—how can I tell them that they are?

MAN. Surely you're not narrow-minded, Agnes?

(She shrugs, not quite sure.)

The ugly, the pimply, the crippled, the fat. Do you wish to get on in this world? Tell them they're handsome.

AGNES. Will they believe it?

MAN. They will believe it because they've always known it. Every man, even the ugliest, feels in his heart a secret alliance with beauty. When you tell him he's handsome, he will simply hear outwardly the voice he has been listening to inwardly all his life. And those who believe it the least will be the most grateful. No matter how ugly they may have thought themselves, the moment they find a woman who thinks them handsome, they grapple her to their hearts with hooks of steel. For them, she is the magic glass of truth, the princess of an enchanted world. When you see a woman who can go nowhere without a staff of admirers, it is not so much because they think she is beautiful, it is because she has told them they are handsome.

AGNES. There are woman then who already know this secret?

MAN. Yes. But they know it without really knowing it. And usually they evade the issue, they go beside the point. They tell the hunchback he is generous, the wall-eyed that he's strong. There's no profit in that. I've seen a woman throw away a cool million in diamonds and emeralds because she told a clubfooted lover that he walked swiftly, when all he wanted to hear was—you know what. And now—to work. The President is in every day to those who come to tell him he's handsome.

AGNES. I'd better come back another day. I have to have training. I have a cousin who's not at all bad-looking— I'll practice on him tomorrow, and then the next day I'll—

MAN. You can practice right now. On the receptionist.

AGNES. That monster?

MAN. The monster is perfect for your purpose. After that, the Vice President. I know him. He's even better. Then the President.

(The VICE PRESIDENT'S *door opens. The* CLERK *comes in.)*

CLERK. *(Into the doorway)* Very good, sir.
VOICE. And another thing—
CLERK. *(Turns)* Yes sir?
VOICE. When the Chairman of the Board—

THE APOLLO OF BELLAC 13

(CLERK *goes back in and closes the door.*)

AGNES. No, I can't!
MAN. *(Indicating the bust of Archimedes at rear)* Begin with this bust then.
AGNES. Whose is it?
MAN. What does it matter? It's the bust of a man. It's all ears. Speak!
AGNES. *(Shuddering)* It has a beard.
MAN. Begin with what you like. With this chair. With this clock.
AGNES. They're not listening.
MAN. This fly, then. See? He's on your glove. He's listening.
AGNES. Is he a male?
MAN. Yes. Speak. Tell him.
AGNES. *(With an effort)* How handsome he is!
MAN. No, no, no. Say it to him.
AGNES. How handsome you are!
MAN. You see? He's twirling his moustache. Go on. More. More. What is a fly especially vain of?
AGNES. His wings? His eyes?
MAN. That's it. Tell him.
AGNES. How beautiful your wings are, beautiful fly! They sparkle in the sun like jewels. And your eyes—so large, so sad, so sensitive!
MAN. Splendid. Shoo him away now. Here comes the clerk.
AGNES. He won't go. He's clinging to me.
MAN. Naturally.
AGNES. *(To the fly)* You're bowlegged. *(She smiles)* He's gone.
MAN. You see? And now—
    (The VICE PRESIDENT'S *door open slowly.)*
Here he comes.
AGNES. *(In panic)* What must I say?
MAN. "How handsome you are."

(CLERK *comes in and walks to his desk.* MAN *disappears behind the bust of Archimedes.*)

AGNES. *(After an agony of indecision)* How handsome you are!
CLERK. *(Stops dead)* What?
AGNES. I said, how handsome you are!
CLERK. Do you get this way often?
AGNES. It's the first time in my life that I've ever—
CLERK. *(Finishing the sentence for her)* Called a chimpanzee handsome? Thanks for the compliment. But—why?
AGNES. You're right. Handsome is not the word. I should have said beautiful. Because, mind you, I never judge a face by the shape of the nose or the arch of the brow. To me, what counts is the ensemble.
CLERK. So what you're telling me is: your features are ugly, but they go beautifully together. Is that it?
AGNES. It serves me right. Very well— It's the first time I've ever told a man he was handsome. And it's going to be the last.
CLERK. Now don't get excited, please. I know girls. At your age a girl doesn't calculate; she says whatever comes into her head. I know you meant it. Only—why did you say it so badly?

(MAN *sticks his head out and makes a face at* AGNES *behind the* CLERK's *back.*)

AGNES. *(To the* MAN*)* Did I say it badly? *(To the* CLERK, *who thinks it is said to him)* I thought you were handsome. I may have been wrong.
CLERK. Women are blind as bats. Even if there were something good about me, they'd never see it. What's so good about me? My face? God, no. My figure? Not at all. Only my shadow. But of course you didn't notice that.
AGNES. Is that what you think? And when you leaned over to close the window, I suppose your shadow didn't

lean over with you? And when you walked into the Vice President's office, did you put your shadow away in a drawer? *(She strokes his shadow with her hand)* How could I help noticing a shadow like that?

CLERK. You notice it now because I direct your attention to it.

AGNES. Have it your way. I thought I was looking at you, but what I saw was your shadow.

CLERK. Then you shouldn't say, what a handsome man. You should say, what a handsome shadow.

(He opens the window, the room is filled with MUSIC. It is still "La Seine.")

AGNES. From now on, I shall say no more about it.

CLERK. *(Returning to desk)* Don't be angry, my dear. It's only because I'm a man of years and I have a right to warn you. I have a daughter of your age. I know what girls are. One day they see a fine shadow, and at once their heads are turned, the silly geese, and they think the man himself is handsome. Oh, I don't deny it, it's a rare thing, a fine shadow. And believe me it lasts —you don't keep your hair, you don't keep your skin, but your shadow lasts all your life. Even longer, they say. But that's not the point. These little fools invariably insist on confusing the shadow with the man, and if the idiot lets himself be talked into it, in a moment it's all over and they've ruined their lives for nothing, the nitwits. No, my dear. Heed an old man's warning. You can't live your life among shadows.

(MAN sticks out his head and lifts an admonishing finger.)

AGNES. How handsome you are!

CLERK. You know why? It's because when I'm angry I show my teeth. And the fact is, they are rather good. My dentist says they're perfect. It's no credit to me— It's because I eat hard foods. And when you—

(The BUZZER sounds again.)

Ah—the Vice President needs me again. Wait just a minute, my dear. I'll make sure that he sees you at once. I'll say it's my niece.

AGNES. *(As he bends over to close a drawer)* How beautiful it is, your shadow, when it leans over. One would say it belonged to Rodin's Thinker!

CLERK. *(Delighted)* Come, now, that will do. If you were my daughter, I'd give you a good slap on the—. Sit down a minute. I'll get him for you. *(Crosses to the VICE PRESIDENT'S door and goes out.)*

(MAN *comes out from behind the bust. The MUSIC stops.*)

MAN. Well, it's a start.

AGNES. I think I'm better with flies.

MAN. Because in your mind the idea of beauty is inseparable from the idea of the caress. Women have no sense of the abstract—a woman admiring the sky is a woman caressing the sky. In a woman's mind beauty is something she needs to touch. And you didn't want to touch the clerk, not even his shadow.

AGNES. No.

MAN. With my method, it's not your hands that must speak, nor your cheek, nor your lips—. It's your brain.

AGNES. I had a narrow squeak. I almost lost him.

MAN. Yes, he had you there with his shadow. You're not ready to tackle a Vice President. No. Not yet.

AGNES. But there's no time. What shall I do?

MAN. Practice. Practice on me.

AGNES. You expect me to tell you you're handsome?

MAN. Is it so difficult?

AGNES. Not at all. Only—

MAN. Think. Think before you speak.

AGNES. Oh, you're not bad at all, you know, when you tease one like this.

MAN. Very feeble. Why when I tease one like this? The rest of the time, I'm not handsome?

AGNES. Oh yes. Always. Always.

THE APOLLO OF BELLAC

MAN. Better. Now it's no longer your hands that are speaking.

AGNES. With you, all the same, they murmur a little something.

MAN. Good.

AGNES. The mass of your body is beautiful. The outline is beautiful. The face matters little.

MAN. What nonsense is this? My face matters little?

AGNES. *(Recovering quickly)* No more than the face of Rodin's Thinker.

MAN. In his case, doubtless the feet have more importance. Look here, Agnes, these little allusions to famous statues are ingenious. But is Rodin's Thinker the only one you know?

AGNES. Except for the Venus of Milo. But she wouldn't be much use to me with men.

MAN. That remains to be seen. In any case, we'd better extend your repertory. Forget The Thinker. Michelangelo's David is very good. Or his Moses. But best of all—the Apollo of Bellac—

AGNES. The Apollo of Bellac?

MAN. It doesn't exist. It will do perfectly.

AGNES. What does it look like?

MAN. A little like me, I think. I too come from Bellac. It's a little town in Limousin. I was born there.

AGNES. But they say the men of Limousin are so ugly. How does it happen that you are so handsome?

MAN. My father was a very handsome man, and he— Oh-oh. Good for you. *(He applauds.)*

AGNES. *(Pursuing her advantage)* Oh never! Not with you! You taught me the secret. With you I could be no other than honest.

MAN. At last. You understand.

(The Vice PRESIDENT'S *door opens.)*
Here we are. *(Goes behind the bust.)*

CLERK. *(Comes in, smiling tenderly)* The Vice President will be out in a moment, my dear. No need to put yourself out. A shadow like his, you may see every

day—in the zoo. *(He takes some papers from his desk and goes into where the Directors will meet.)*
AGNES. *(Whispers)* Help! Help!
(MAN thrusts his head out.)
I feel faint!
MAN. Practice. Practice.
AGNES. *(Desperately)* On whom? On what?
MAN. On anything. The telephone.
AGNES. *(She speaks to the telephone)* How handsome you are, my little telephone! *(She strokes it gently.)*
MAN. No! Not with the hands.
AGNES. But it's so much easier that way.
MAN. I know. Try the chandelier. That's one thing you can't touch.
AGNES. How handsome you are, my little, my great chandelier!
(The MUSIC begins again. Another tune.)
Only when you're all lit up? Oh, don't say that. Other chandeliers, yes. Street lamps, store-fixtures, yes. Not you. See—you are full of sunshine. You are the chandelier of the sun. A desk lamp needs to be lit. A planet needs to be lit. But you have radiance of your own. You are as beautiful as a galaxy of stars, even more beautiful, for a galaxy is only an imitation chandelier, a cluster of uncertain lights swinging precariously in the eternal darkness. But you are a creature of crystal with limbs of ivory and gold, a living miracle!

(The chandelier LIGHTS up by itself.)

MAN. Bravo!
VICE PRESIDENT. *(The door opens. The VICE PRESIDENT comes in. His manner is important. His face is that of a gargoyle)* My dear young lady, I have exactly two minutes to give you. *(He crosses to close the window.)*
AGNES. *(Whispering in awe)* Oh!

THE APOLLO OF BELLAC

VICE PRESIDENT. *(Stops and turns)* Why do you stare at me like that? You've seen me before?

AGNES. *(In a tone of wonder)* No! On the contrary.

VICE PRESIDENT. And what does that mean, no, on the contrary?

AGNES. I was expecting to see the usual Vice President, stoop-shouldered, paunchy, bald— And all at once, I see you!

(VICE PRESIDENT *freezes in his tracks.* MAN *thrusts out his head. He raises a warning finger.*)

(Hastily) How handsome you are!

VICE PRESIDENT. What? *(He turns.)*

AGNES. Nothing. I beg your pardon.

VICE PRESIDENT. I heard you distinctly. You said I was handsome. Don't deny it. *(He steps closer to her)* *(MUSIC swells up.)*
You know, it gave me rather a shock to hear you say it. However, it can't be true. If I were really—what you said—wouldn't some woman have told me before this?

AGNES. Oh, the fools! The fools!

VICE PRESIDENT. Whom are you calling fools, Mademoiselle? My sister, my mother, my niece?

AGNES. *(Giving up all at once. In a formal tone)* Mr. Vice President, the truth is I am looking for a position. And I happened to hear through a friend of one of your directors, Mr. Lepédura—

(MAN *thrusts out his head.*)

VICE PRESIDENT. Never mind Monsieur Lepédura. We are discussing me. As you probably know, I am one of the world's authorities in the fields of dreams. It is I who work with those who are able to invent only while they sleep, and I have been able to extract from their dreams such extraordinary devices as the book that reads itself and the adjustable Martini, wonders of modern science which without my help would have remained mere figments of the imagination. If you appeared to me in a dream and told me I was handsome, I should have understood at once. But we are in a waking state, or are we? One moment. *(He pinches himself)* Ow! I am awake. Permit me. *(Pinches her.)*

AGNES. Ow!

VICE PRESIDENT. We're not dreaming, Mademoiselle. And now, my dear— *(He takes her hand)* Why did you say I was handsome? To flatter me?—I can see you are incapable of such baseness. To make fun of me? No— your eye is gentle, your lips attract— Why did you say it, Mademoiselle?

AGNES. I say you are handsome because you are handsome. If your mother finds you ugly that's not my concern.

VICE PRESIDENT. I cannot permit you to form so low an opinion of my mother's taste. Even when I was a boy, my mother used to say I had the hands of an artist.

AGNES. If your niece prefers Charles Boyer—

VICE PRESIDENT. My niece? Only yesterday at dinner she was saying that my eyebrows could have been drawn by El Greco.

AGNES. If your sister—

VICE PRESIDENT. My sister has never quite admitted that I am handsome, no, but she has always said that there was something distinctive about my face. A friend of hers, a history teacher, told her it's because in certain lights, I resemble Lodovico Sforza. *(He makes a deprecating gesture.)*

AGNES. Lodovico Sforza? Never. The Apollo of Bellac, yes.

VICE PRESIDENT. The Apollo of Bellac?

AGNES. Wouldn't you say? Quite objectively?

VICE PRESIDENT. Well—if you really think so—perhaps just a little. Although Lodovico Sforza, you know —I've seen engravings—

AGNES. When I say the Apollo of Bellac, I mean, naturally, the Apollo of Bellac in a beautifuly tailored suit. You see, I am frank. I say what I think. Yes, Mr. Vice President. You have the fault of all really handsome men—you dress carelessly.

THE APOLLO OF BELLAC

VICE PRESIDENT. *(Smiling)* What insolence! And this from a girl who tells every man she meets that he's handsome!

AGNES. I have said that to two men only in all my life. You are the second.

(CLERK *comes in.*)

VICE PRESIDENT. What is it? Don't you see I'm busy?

CLERK. The Directors are on the way up, sir. It's time for the meeting.

VICE PRESIDENT. I'll be right in.

(CLERK *goes into the Directors' room.*)

I'm sorry, Mademoiselle. I must go to this meeting. But we must certainly continue this wonderful conversation. Won't you come back and lunch with me? You know, my secretary is impossible. I'm having her transfered to the sales department. Now you're a first-rate typist, I'm told—

AGNES. I don't type. I play the piano.

VICE PRESIDENT. Ah, that's wonderful. And you take dictation?

AGNES. In longhand, yes.

VICE PRESIDENT. That's much the best way. That gives one time to think. Would you like to be my secretary?

AGNES. On one condition.

VICE PRESIDENT. A condition?

AGNES. On condition that you never wear this awful jacket again. When I think of these wonderful shoulders in that ill-fitting suit—!

VICE PRESIDENT. I have a beautiful blue silk suit. But it's for summer— It's a little light for the season.

AGNES. As you please.

VICE PRESIDENT. I'll wear it tomorrow.

AGNES. Good-bye.

VICE PRESIDENT. Don't forget. Lunch. *(He goes out, smiling, by way of the door to the Directors' room. The Street MUSIC stops.)*

(MAN *peers out from behind the bust.*)

AGNES. I kept my hands behind my back the whole time. I pretended I had no hands. Now I can hardly move my fingers.
MAN. Here come the rest of the apes. Go to work.
AGNES. On the first?
MAN. On all. One after the other.
AGNES. But—

(CLERK *throws open the doors of the Directors' room. The street MUSIC starts again. We have a glimpse of the Directors' table with chairs pulled back ready to receive the Directors. The* VICE PRESIDENT *is seen inside. He is posturing in front of a bookcase in the glass door of which he sees himself reflected, and he is trying vainly to give a smartly tailored appearance to his coat.* CLERK *glances at him in astonishment, then he stands by the outer door to announce the Directors as they appear. They come in through the outer door and cross the length of the reception room, one by one in time to the music, which is a waltz.*)

CLERK. Mr. Cracheton.

(MR. CRACHETON *comes in, a lugubrious type, stiff and melancholy.*)

AGNES. How handsome he is!
CRACHETON. *(He snaps his head about as if shot. His expression changes. He smiles. In a low voice)* Charming girl! *(He goes into the Directors' room, looking all the while over his shoulder.)*
CLERK. Mr. Lepédura.
LEPÉDURA. *(Appears. He has a face full of suspicion and worry. As he passes* AGNES, *he tips his derby perfunctorily, recognizing her)* Good morning.
AGNES. How handsome you are!

LEPÉDURA. *(Stops dead)* Who says so?
AGNES. Your wife's friend, the Baroness Chagrobis. She thinks you're wonderful.
LEPÉDURA. *(A changed man, gallant and charming)* She thinks I'm wonderful? Well, well, give her my love when you see her. And tell her I mean to call her up shortly myself. She has a pretty thin time of it with the Baron, you know. We have to be nice to her. Is she still at the same address?
AGNES. Oh yes. I'll tell her you're as handsome as ever.
LEPÉDURA. Now don't exaggerate, my dear. We don't want to disappoint her. *(He gives her a radiant smile, and goes in, fully six inches taller and many pounds lighter. To the* CLERK*)* Delightful girl!
CLERK. Mr. Rasemutte and Mr. Schultz.

(They enter together, Mutt and Jeff.)

AGNES. How handsome he is!

(BOTH *stop as if at a signal.)*

RASEMUTTE. To which of us, Mademoiselle—
SCHULTZ. —Do you refer?
AGNES. Look at each other. You will see.

(They look at each other anxiously, and BOTH *smile radiantly.)*

RASEMUTTE. Charming creature!
SCHULTZ. Lovely girl!

(SCHULTZ *offers* RASEMUTTE *his arm, They walk into the Directors' room arm in arm like characters in "Alt Wien."* CLERK *blows* AGNES *a kiss, follows them in and closes the doors behind them.* MAN *pokes his head out from behind Archimedes. He shakes his head ruefully.)*

AGNES. I'm not doing it well? You're sad?
MAN. You're doing it much too well. I'm frightened.
AGNES. You?
MAN. Like Frankenstein.

(The door of the Directors' room is flung open.)

CLERK. The President!

(As the PRESIDENT enters the room, we catch a glimpse of the DIRECTORS. Each has a mirror in his hand. While one combs his hair into waves, another settles his tie. Another preens his whiskers. The VICE PRESIDENT has taken off his jacket.)

PRESIDENT. So you're the cause of it all, Miss—Miss—?
AGNES. Agnes.

PRESIDENT. Miss Agnes, for fifteen years this organization has been steeped in melancholy, jealousy and suspicion. And now suddenly this morning, everything is changed. My reception clerk, ordinarily a species of hyena—
  (The CLERK smiles affably.)
has become so affable he even bows to his own shadow on the wall—
  (CLERK contemplates his silhouette in the sunshine with a nod of approval. It nods back.)
The First Vice President, whose reputation for stuffiness and formality has never been seriously challenged, insists on sitting at the Directors' Meeting in his shirtsleeves, God knows why. In the Directors' Room, around the table, mirrors flash like sunbeams in a forest, and my Directors gaze into them with rapture. Mr. Lepédura contemplates with joy the Adam's apple of Mr. Lepédura. Mr. Rasemutte stares with pride at the nose of Mr. Rasemutte. They are all in love with themselves and with each other. How in the world did you

bring about this miracle, Miss Agnes? What was it you said to them?

AGNES. How handsome you are!

PRESIDENT. I beg your pardon?

AGNES. I said to them, to each of them, "How handsome you are!"

PRESIDENT. Ah! You conveyed it to them subtly by means of a smile, a wink, a promise—

AGNES. I said it in a loud clear voice. Like this: How handsome you are!

(In the Directors' Room, all heads turn suddenly. CLERK closes the doors.)

PRESIDENT. I see. Like a child winding up a mechanical doll. Well, well! No wonder my mannikins are quivering with the joy of life.
(There is a round of applause from the Directors' Room.)
Listen to that. It's Mr. Cracheton proposing the purchase of a new three-way mirror for the men's room. Miss Agnes, I thank you. You have made a wonderful discovery.

AGNES. *(Modestly)* Oh, it was nothing.

PRESIDENT. And the President? How does it happen that you don't tell the President?

AGNES. How handsome he is?

PRESIDENT. He's not worth the trouble, is that it?
(She looks at him with a smile full of meaning.)
You've had enough of masculine vanity for one morning?

AGNES. Oh, Mr. President—you know the reason as well as I.

PRESIDENT. No. I assure you.

AGNES. But—I don't need to tell *you*. You *are* handsome.

PRESIDENT. *(Seriously)* Would you mind repeating that?

AGNES. You are handsome.

PRESIDENT. Think carefully, Miss Agnes. This is a serious matter. Are you quite sure that to you I seem handsome?

AGNES. You don't seem handsome. You are handsome.

PRESIDENT. You would be ready to repeat that before witnesses? Think. Much depends upon your answer. I have grave decisions to make today, and the outcome depends entirely upon you. Have you thought? Are you still of the same opinion?

AGNES. Completely.

PRESIDENT. Thank heaven. *(He goes to his private door, opens it and calls)* Chevredent!

(CHEVREDENT *comes in. She is a thin, sour woman with an insolent air. Her nose is pinched. Her chin is high. Her hair is drawn up tightly. When she opens her mouth she appears to be about to bite.)*

CHEVREDENT. Yes? *(She looks at* AGNES *and sniffs audibly.)*

PRESIDENT. Chevredent, how long have you been my private secretary?

CHEVREDENT. Three years and two months. Why?

PRESIDENT. In all that time there has never been a morning when the prospect of finding you in my office has not made me shudder.

CHEVREDENT. Thanks very much. Same to you.

PRESIDENT. I wouldn't have put up with you for ten minutes if it had ever occurred to me that I was handsome.

CHEVREDENT. Ha-ha.

PRESIDENT. But because I thought I was ugly, I took your meanness for generosity. Because I thought I was ugly, I assumed that your evil temper concealed a good heart. I thought it was kind of you even to look at me. For I am ugly, am I not?

(CHEVREDENT *sneers maliciously.*)

Thank you. And now listen to me. This young lady

seems to be far better equipped to see than you. Her eyelids are not red like yours, her pupils are clear, her glance is limpid. Miss Agnes, look at me. Am I ugly?

AGNES. You are beautiful.

(CHEVREDENT *shrugs.*)

PRESIDENT. This young lady's disinterested appraisal of my manly charms has no effect on your opinion?

CHEVREDENT. I never heard such rubbish in my life!

PRESIDENT. Quite so. Well, here is the problem that confronts us. I have the choice of spending my working time with an ugly old shrew who thinks I'm hideous or a delightful young girl who thinks I'm handsome. What do you advise?

CHEVREDENT. You intend to replace me with this little fool?

PRESIDENT. At once.

CHEVREDENT. We'll soon see about that, Mr. President. You may have forgotten, but your wife is inside in your office reading your mail. She should know about this.

PRESIDENT. She should. Tell her.

CHEVREDENT. With pleasure. *(She rushes into the President's office, slamming the door after her.)*

AGNES. I'm terribly sorry, Mr. President.

PRESIDENT. My dear, you come like an angel from heaven at the critical moment of my life. Today is my fifteenth wedding anniversary. My wife, with whose fury Chevredent threatens us, is going to celebrate the occasion by lunching with my Directors. I am going to present her with a gift. A diamond. *(He takes out a case and opens it)* Like it?

AGNES. How handsome it is!

PRESIDENT. Extraordinary! You praised the diamond in exactly the same tone you used for me. Is it yellow by any chance? Is it flawed?

AGNES. It is beautiful. Like you.

PRESIDENT. *(His door opens)* We are about to

become less so, both of us. *(He puts the case in his pocket)* Here is my wife.

THERESE. (THERESE, *the blonde lady, comes in with icy majesty. She looks* AGNES *up and down)* So.

PRESIDENT. Therese, my dear, permit me to present—

THERESE. Quite unnecessary. That will be all, Mademoiselle. You may go.

PRESIDENT. Agnes is staying, my dear. She is replacing Chevredent.

THERESE. Agnes! So she is already Agnes!

PRESIDENT. Why not?

THERESE. And why is Agnes replacing Chevredent?

PRESIDENT. Because she thinks I'm handsome.

THERESE. Are you mad?

PRESIDENT. No. Handsome.

THERESE. *(To* AGNES) You think he's handsome?

AGNES. Oh yes.

THERESE. He makes you think of Galahad? Of Lancelot?

AGNES. Oh no. His type is classic. The Apollo of Bellac.

THERESE. The Apollo of Bellac?

PRESIDENT. Have you ever stopped to wonder, Therese, why the good Lord made women? Obviously they were not torn from our ribs in order to make life a torment for us. Women exist in order to tell men they are handsome. And those who say it the most are those who are most beautiful. Agnes tells me I'm handsome. It's because she's beautiful. You tell me I'm ugly. Why?

MAN. *(Appears. He applauds)* Bravo! Bravo!

THERESE. Who is this maniac?

MAN. When one hears a voice which goes to the very heart of humanity, it is impossible to keep silent.

PRESIDENT. My friend—

MAN. From the time of Adam and Eve, of Samson and Delilah, of Antony and Cleopatra, the problem of man and woman has made an impenetrable barrier between man and woman. If, as it seems, we are able

THE APOLLO OF BELLAC

to solve this problem once and for all, it will be a work of immeasurable benefit to the human race.

THERESE. And you think we're getting somewhere with it today, is that it?

MAN. Oh, yes.

THERESE. You don't think the final solution could be deferred until tomorrow?

MAN. Till tomorrow? When the President has just posed the problem so beautifully?

AGNES. So beautifully!

THERESE. The beautiful man poses a beautiful problem, eh, Mademoiselle?

AGNES. I didn't say it. But I can say it. I say what I think.

THERESE. Little cheat!

PRESIDENT. I forbid you to insult Agnes!

THERESE. It's she who insults me!

PRESIDENT. When I'm called handsome, it's an insult to you—is that it?

THERESE. I'm no liar.

PRESIDENT. No. You show us the bottom of your heart.

MAN. Agnes is telling the President the truth, Madame. Just as Cleopatra told the truth, just as Isolt told the truth. The truth about men is, they are beautiful, every last one of them; and your husband is right, Madame, the woman who tells it to them never lies.

THERESE. So I am the liar!

MAN. *(Gently)* It's only because you don't see clearly. All you have to do to see the beauty of men is to watch as they breathe and move their limbs. Each has his special grace. His beauty of body. The heavy ones—how powerfully they hold the ground! The light ones—how well they hang from the sky! His beauty of position. A hunchback on the ridge of Notre Dame makes a masterpiece of Gothic sculpture. All you have to do is to get him up there. And, finally, his beauty of function. The steamfitter has the beauty of a steamfitter. The president has the beauty of a president. There is ugliness only when these beauties become confused—when the steamfitter has the beauty of a president, the president the beauty of a steamfitter.

AGNES. But there is no such confusion here.

THERESE. No. He has the beauty of a garbageman.

PRESIDENT. Thanks very much.

THERESE. My dear, I have known you too long to deceive you. You have many good qualities. But you're ugly.

PRESIDENT. Quiet!

THERESE. Yes. Yes. Ugly! This girl, whatever her motives, is just able to force her lips to whisper her lies. But with every part of me—my heart, my lungs, my arms, my eyes—I scream the truth at you. My legs! You're ugly! Do you hear?

PRESIDENT. I've heard nothing else for years.

THERESE. Because it's true.

MAN. There. And at last she's confessed.

THERESE. Confessed what? What have I confessed?

MAN. Your crime, Madame. You have injured this man. How could you expect him to be handsome in an environment that screamed at him constantly that he was ugly?

PRESIDENT. Ah! Now I understand!

THERESE. What do you understand? What's the matter with you all? What have I done?

PRESIDENT. Now I understand why I am always embarrassed not only in your presence, but in the presence of everything that belongs to you.

THERESE. Do you know what he is talking about?

PRESIDENT. The sight of your skirt on the back of a chair shortens my spine by three inches. Can you expect me to stand up like a man when you come in? Your stockings on the bureau tell me that I'm knock-kneed and thick-ankled. Is it any wonder if I stumble? Your nail file on my desk hisses at me that my fingers are thick and my gestures clumsy. What do you expect of me after that? And your onyx clock with the Dying Gaul on the mantelpiece—no wonder I always shiver when I go near the fire. Imagine—for fifteen years that Dying Gaul has been sneering at me in my own house, and I never realized why I was uncomfortable. Well, at last I understand. And this very evening—

THERESE. Don't you dare!

PRESIDENT. This very evening your Dying Gaul shall die. You will find him in the garbage with the rest of the conspiracy. Your Dresden china shepherd, your Arab sheik, your directoire chairs with their scratchy bottoms—

THERESE. Those chairs belonged to my grandmother!

PRESIDENT. From now on they belong to the garbage. What are your chairs covered with, Agnes?

AGNES. Yellow satin.

PRESIDENT. I knew it. And the statues on your table?

AGNES. There is only a bowl of fresh flowers on my table. Today it is white carnations.

PRESIDENT. Of course. And over your fireplace?

AGNES. A mirror.

PRESIDENT. Naturally.

THERESE. I warn you, if you so much as touch my chairs, I'll leave you forever.

PRESIDENT. As you please, my dear.

THERESE. I see. So this is my anniversary gift after fifteen years of devotion. Very well. Only tell me, what have you to complain of? In all these years has it ever happened that your roast was too rare? Did I ever give you your coffee too cold, too hot, too light, too sweet? Thanks to me, you are known as a man whose handkerchief is always fresh, whose socks are always new. Have you ever known what it was to have a hole in your toe? Has anyone ever seen a spot on your vest? And yet how you splash in your gravy, my friend! How you go through your socks!

PRESIDENT. Tell me one thing. Do you say I am ugly because you think I am ugly or merely to spite me?

THERESE. Because you are ugly.

PRESIDENT. Thank you, Therese. Go on.

THERESE. Then this woman appears. And at the first

glance we can guess the fate of the unhappy creature who marries her. We see it all—the slippers with the inner sole curled up in a scroll. The nightly battle over the newspaper. The pajamas without buttons and always too small. The headaches without aspirin, the soup without salt, the shower without towels—

PRESIDENT. Agnes, one question. Do you tell me I'm handsome because you think I'm handsome or only to make fun of me?

AGNES. Because you're handsome.

PRESIDENT. Thank you, Agnes.

THERESE. You mean because he's rich.

AGNES. If he were the richest man in the world, I'd still say he was handsome.

THERESE. Very well. Marry her if she thinks you're so handsome. Well? What are you waiting for?

PRESIDENT. Nothing.

THERESE. Take him, you, with my compliments. After fifteen years I've had enough. If you like to hear snoring at night—

AGNES. You snore? How wonderful!

THERESE. If you like bony knees—

AGNES. I like legs that have character.

THERESE. Look at that face! Now tell me he has the brow of a Roman Senator.

AGNES. No, Madame.

THERESE. No?

AGNES. The brow of a king.

THERESE. I give up. Goodbye.

PRESIDENT. Goodbye, my love.

(THERESE *rushes out through outer door.*)

And now, Agnes, in token of a happy future, accept this diamond. For me, one life has ended, and another begins.

(CLERK *comes in and signs to him.*)

Forgive me just one moment, Agnes. I must address the Directors. The Chairman of the Board is evidently not coming. I'll be right back. *(He crosses to the door. To the* CLERK*)* Send down to the florist. I want all the

white carnations he has. Agnes, you have made me the happiest of men.
AGNES. The handsomest.

(The PRESIDENT goes out by his door, the CLERK by outer door.)

MAN. Well, there you are, my dear. You have everything—a job, a husband and a diamond. I can leave?
AGNES. Oh no!

(The street MUSIC starts afresh.)

MAN. But what more do you want?
AGNES. Look at me. I have changed—haven't I?
MAN. Perhaps just a little. That can't be helped.
AGNES. It's your fault. I have told so many lies! I must tell the truth at last or I shall burst!
MAN. What truth do you want to tell?
AGNES. I want to tell someone who is really beautiful that he is beautiful. I want to tell the most beautiful man in the world that he is the most beautiful man in the world.
MAN. And to caress him, perhaps, just a little?
AGNES. Just a little.
MAN. There is the Apollo of Bellac.
AGNES. He doesn't exist.
MAN. What does it matter whether or not he exists? His beauty is the supreme beauty. Tell him.
AGNES. I can't. Unless I touch a thing I don't see it. You know that. I have no imagination.
MAN. Close your eyes.
AGNES. *(Closes them)* Yes?
MAN. Suppose, Agnes, it were the God of Beauty himself who visited you this morning. Don't be astonished. Perhaps it's true. Where else could this terrible power have come from? Or this extraordinary emotion you feel? Or this sense of oppression? And suppose that now the god reveals himself?

AGNES. It is you?
MAN. Don't open your eyes. Suppose I stand before you now in all my truth and all my splendor.
AGNES. I see you.
MAN. Call me thou.
AGNES. I see thee.
MAN. How do I seem?
AGNES. You seem—
MAN. I am taller than mortal men. My head is small and fringed with golden ringlets. From the line of my shoulders, the geometricians derived the idea of the square. From my eyebrows the bowmen drew the concept of the arc. I am nude and this nudity inspired in the musicians the idea of harmony.
AGNES. Your heels are winged, are they not?
MAN. They are not. You are thinking of the Hermes of St. Yrieix.
AGNES. I don't see your eyes.
MAN. As for the eyes, it's as well you don't see them. The eyes of beauty are implacable. My eyeballs are silver. My pupils are graphite. From the eyes of beauty poets derived the idea of death. But the feet of beauty are enchanting. They are not feet that touch the ground. They are never soiled and never captive. The toes are slender, and from them artists derived the idea of symmetry. Do you see me now?
AGNES. You dazzle my eyes.
MAN. But your heart sees me.
AGNES. I'm not so sure. Do not count on me too much, God of Beauty. My life is small. My days are long, and when I come back to my room each evening, there are five flights to climb in the greasy twilight amid smells of cooking. These five flights mark the beginning and the end of every event of my life, and oh, if you knew, Apollo, how lonely I am! Sometimes I find a cat waiting in a doorway. I kneel and stroke it for a moment, we purr together and it fills the rest of my day with joy. Sometimes I see a milk bottle that has fallen on its side. I set it right and the gesture comforts

me. If I smell gas in the hallway I run and speak to the janitor. It is so good to speak to someone about something. Between the second story and the third, the steps sag. At this turning one abandons hope. At this turning one loses one's balance, and catches at the bannister, gasping with the anguish of those more fortunate ones who clutch at the rail on the heaving deck of a ship. That is my life, Apollo, a thing of shadows and tortured flesh. That is my conscience, Apollo, a staircase full of stale odors. If I hesitate to see you as you are, O beautiful god, it is because I need so much and I have so little and I must defend myself.

MAN. But I have rescued you, Agnes. You possess the secret.

AGNES. I know. From now on, my staircase will be new and full of light, the treads carpeted in velvet and adorned with initials. But to climb it with you would be unthinkable. Go away, God of Beauty. Leave me for always.

MAN. You wish that?

AGNES. If you were merely a handsome man, Apollo, thick and human in your flesh, with what joy I would take you in my arms! How I would love you! But you are too brilliant and too great for my staircase. I would do better to look at my diamond. Go, Apollo. Go away. Before I open my eyes, I implore you, vanish.

MAN. When I vanish, you will see before you an ordinary creature like yourself, covered with skin, covered with clothes.

AGNES. That is my destiny, and I prefer it. Let me kiss your lips, Apollo. And then—

MAN. *(He kisses her)* Open your eyes, my dear. Apollo is gone. And I am going.

AGNES. How handsome you are!

MAN. Dear Agnes!

AGNES. Don't go. I will make you rich. I will order the President to buy your invention.

MAN. Which one?

AGNES. The Universal Vegetable. There must be a fortune in it.

MAN. I haven't quite got the hang of it yet. The roots don't hold the earth. I'll be back the moment I've perfected it.

AGNES. You promise?

MAN. We shall plant it together. And now—

AGNES. You are really leaving me? You think I shall marry the President?

MAN. No.

AGNES. Why not?

MAN. He's already married. And his wife has learned a lesson. You will see.

AGNES. Then whom shall I marry, if not the President?

CLERK. *(Enters. He crosses to the Directors' Room and throws open the door. Announces)* The Chairman of the Board!

(The CHAIRMAN enters from outer door.)

MAN. *(Whispers)* He is a bachelor.

AGNES. How handsome he is!

MAN. Yes. *(He vanishes.)*

CHAIRMAN. Mademoiselle—

PRESIDENT. *(The PRESIDENT comes in quickly in great excitement)* Agnes! Agnes! A miracle! My wife has just telephoned. I don't know what has come over her. She has thrown out the Dying Gaul and the china shepherd.

AGNES. Give her this diamond.

PRESIDENT. Thank you, Agnes. Thank you.

CHAIRMAN. *(Taking her hand)* And who is this charming girl who gives away diamonds?

AGNES. Her name is Agnes.

CHAIRMAN. Dear Agnes!

PRESIDENT. But what's happened to our friend? He isn't here?

AGNES. He is gone.

PRESIDENT. Call him back. He must have lunch with us. Do you know his name?
AGNES. His first name only. Apollo.
PRESIDENT. *(Runs to the outer door)* Apollo! Apollo!
(The DIRECTORS come in, all adorned with white carnations.)
Gentlemen, gentlemen, let's call him! We can't let him go like that. Apollo!

(They each go to a door or a window save AGNES and the CHAIRMAN who remain standing hand in hand.)

PRESIDENT and DIRECTORS. Apollo! Apollo!
CHAIRMAN. But whom are they shouting at? Is Apollo here?
AGNES. No. He just passed by.

CURTAIN

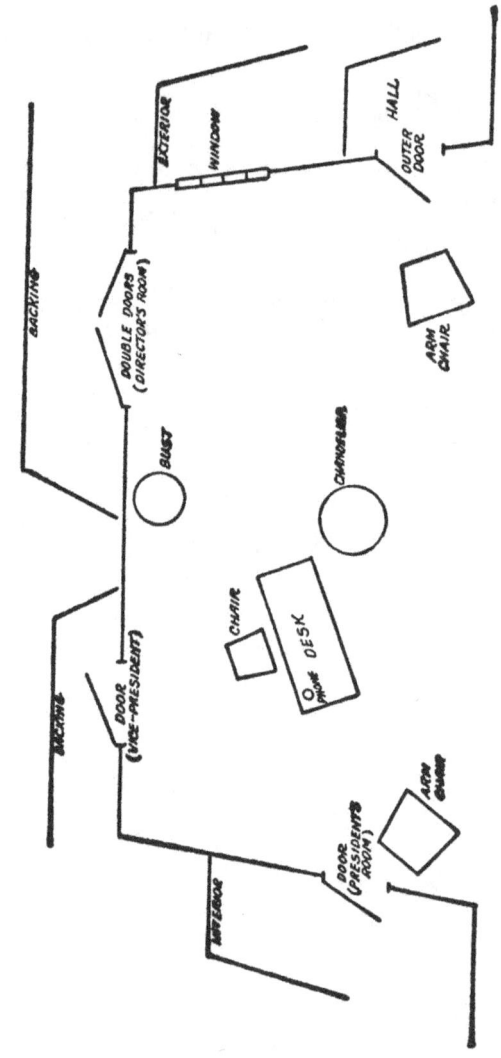

MUSIC USE NOTE

Licensees are solely responsible for obtaining formal written permission from copyright owners to use copyrighted music in the performance of this play and are strongly cautioned to do so. If no such permission is obtained by the licensee, then the licensee must use only original music that the licensee owns and controls. Licensees are solely responsible and liable for all music clearances and shall indemnify the copyright owners of the play(s) and their licensing agent, Samuel French, against any costs, expenses, losses and liabilities arising from the use of music by licensees. Please contact the appropriate music licensing authority in your territory for the rights to any incidental music.

IMPORTANT BILLING AND CREDIT REQUIREMENTS

If you have obtained performance rights to this title, please refer to your licensing agreement for important billing and credit requirements.

www.ingramcontent.com/pod-product-compliance
Lightning Source LLC
Chambersburg PA
CBHW072022290426
44109CB00018B/2320